Making Maps

Ben Nussbaum

※ Smithsonian

Contributing Author

Jennifer Lawson

Consultants

Dan Cole, M.A.
GIS Coordinator and Chief Cartographer
National Museum of Natural History

Sharon Banks
3rd Grade Teacher
Duncan Public Schools

Publishing Credits

Rachelle Cracchiolo, M.S.Ed., *Publisher*
Conni Medina, M.A.Ed., *Managing Editor*
Diana Kenney, M.A.Ed., NBCT, *Content Director*
Véronique Bos, *Creative Director*
Robin Erickson, *Art Director*
Michelle Jovin, M.A., *Associate Editor*
Mindy Duits, *Senior Graphic Designer*
Smithsonian Science Education Center

Image Credits: p.6 (bottom) World History Archive/Alamy; p.8 Library of Congress [G9111.P5 1633 .R7]; p.9 (all) Courtesy University of Minnesota; p.10 Geographicus Rare Antique Maps; p.11 World Digital Library/National Library of Sweden; p.12 (left) Gerry P. Young; p.12 (right) © Smithsonian; pp.14–15 Image courtesy of Submarine Ring of Fire 2012 Exploration, NOAA Vents Program; p.15 Dorling Kindersley/Science Source; p.16 Courtesy of Defense Visual Information Center; pp.16–17 Library of Congress [LC-DIG-ppmsca-03354]; p.18, p.19, pp. 20–21, p.27 (bottom) NASA; p.20 (bottom) Patrick Chapuis/Sygma via Getty Images; p.24 Louise Murray/Science Source; p.25 (top) Ekkasit Keatsirikul/Alamy; p.25 (bottom), p.32 Mike Dotta/Shutterstock; p.31 Library of Congress [G1001 .A4 1544]; all other images from iStock and/or Shutterstock.

Library of Congress Cataloging-in-Publication Data

Names: Nussbaum, Ben, 1975- author.
Title: Making maps / Ben Nussbaum.
Description: Huntington Beach, California : Teacher Created Materials, [2019]
| Audience: Grades: K to Grade 3. | Includes index. |
Identifiers: LCCN 2018030494 (print) | LCCN 2018038536 (ebook) | ISBN
9781493869053 | ISBN 9781493866656
Subjects: LCSH: Maps--Juvenile literature. | Map drawing--Juvenile literature.
Classification: LCC GA130 (ebook) | LCC GA130 ,N87 2019 (print) | DDC
526--dc23
LC record available at https://lccn.loc.gov/2018030494

☀ Smithsonian

© 2019 Smithsonian Institution. The name "Smithsonian"
and the Smithsonian logo are registered trademarks
owned by the Smithsonian Institution.

Teacher Created Materials

5301 Oceanus Drive
Huntington Beach, CA 92649-1030
www.tcmpub.com
ISBN 978-1-4938-6665-6
© 2019 Teacher Created Materials, Inc.

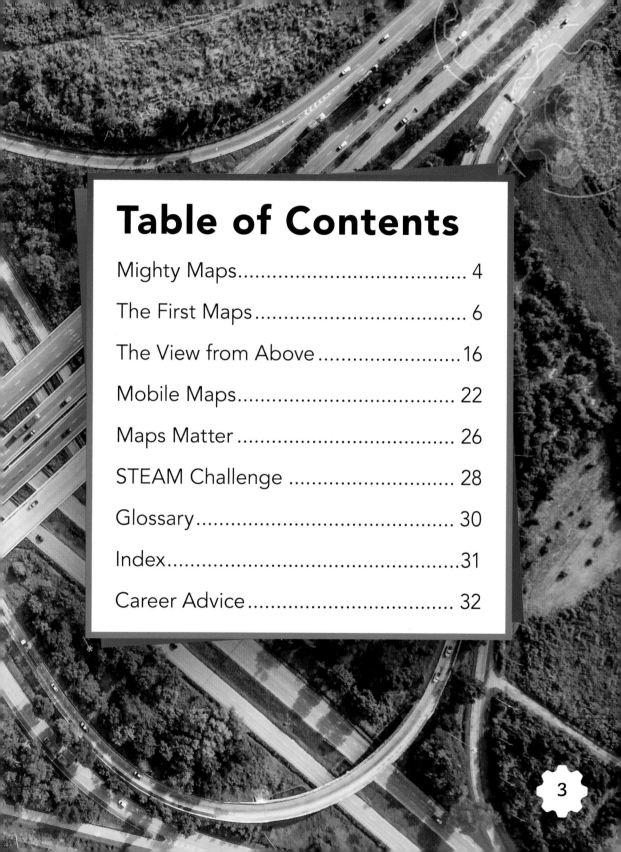

Table of Contents

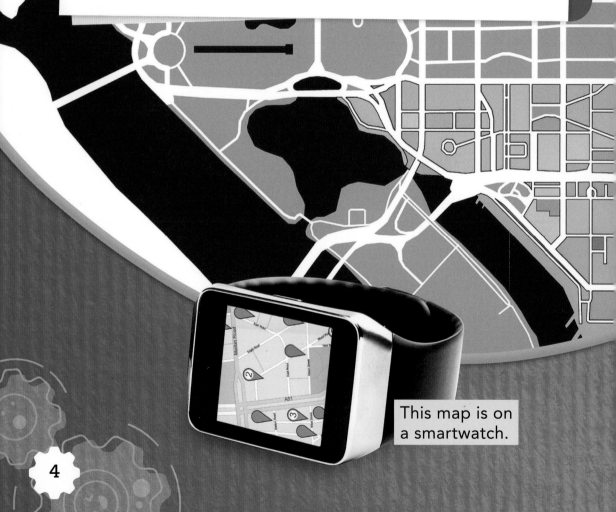

Mighty Maps

Maps tell people which way to turn. They tell ambulance drivers how to find people who need help. Maps can help people save lives.

Maps have been around a long time. They have changed a lot since they were first made. Maps today are small enough to fit in a person's pocket—but they are a big deal.

This map is on a smartwatch.

This map shows streets, water, and green spaces.

This map is on a smartphone.

5

The First Maps

No one knows when the first map was made. It was probably just lines scratched in dirt.

One of the oldest maps that still survives is made from clay. It was created in Babylon, a city from long ago. The map does not have a lot of details. Some places on the map are still around. Some places are not.

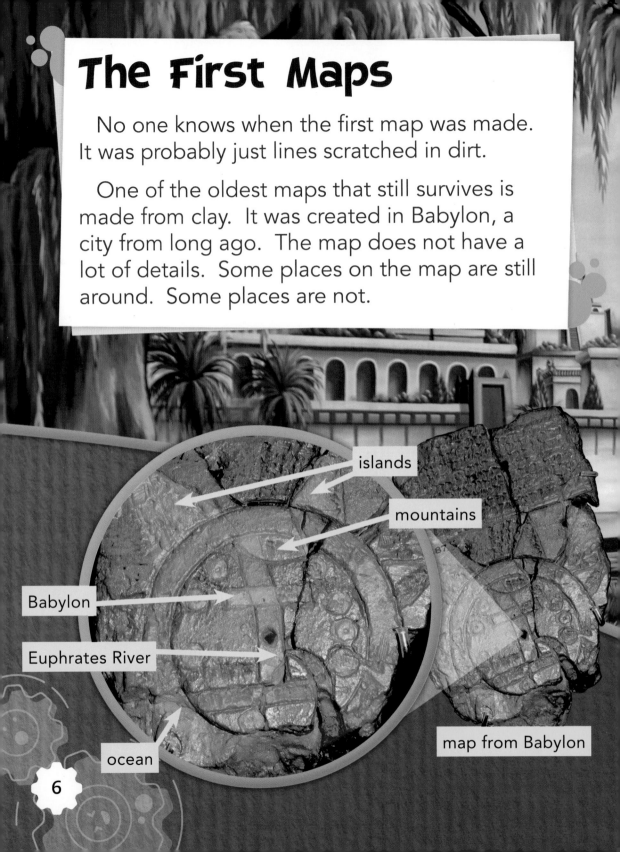

islands

mountains

Babylon

Euphrates River

ocean

map from Babylon

This painting shows what the entrance to Babylon might have looked like.

For many years, there were not a lot of maps. Maps had to be drawn by hand. Most were not very **accurate**.

Maps cost a lot of money to make. They cost a lot of money to buy too. Only rich people could afford maps.

About five hundred years ago, people learned how to print maps. Maps became cheaper to make. They also became more common.

This map of the world was hand-drawn in 1633.

In Europe, many old maps were drawn on animal skins. In China, many old maps were drawn on silk.

Old maps had details drawn on them to tell stories about places.

This map was drawn on animal skin in Spain in 1466.

9

Blank Spaces

Some old maps have blank spaces. People who made the maps did not know what was there. Some places had never been **explored**.

Sometimes, mapmakers drew monsters in places that were still mysteries. Other times, they guessed on what they thought was there. Over the years, maps improved.

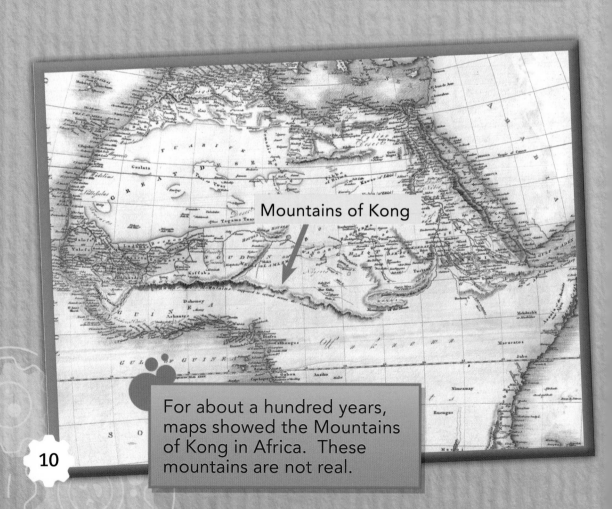

Mountains of Kong

For about a hundred years, maps showed the Mountains of Kong in Africa. These mountains are not real.

This 1572 map shows monsters in the sea below Iceland.

To help mapmakers fill in the blanks, explorers went to new places. They had no maps to help them find their way. So, they took tools to find where they were.

One of the tools explorers still use is called a **quadrant** (KWAH-druhnt). It shows the angle between a person on the ground and the sun or a star. It can show how far north or south a person is. Another mapping tool is a **compass**. It helps people know which way they are going.

A man uses a quadrant.

This quadrant was made in the 1600s.

Finding Direction

The needle on a compass is a magnet. Earth is also a magnet. The north and south poles are the most magnetic parts of Earth. The needle on a compass spins until it points north or south, depending on the type of compass and whether a person is north or south of the equator.

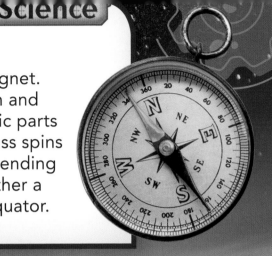

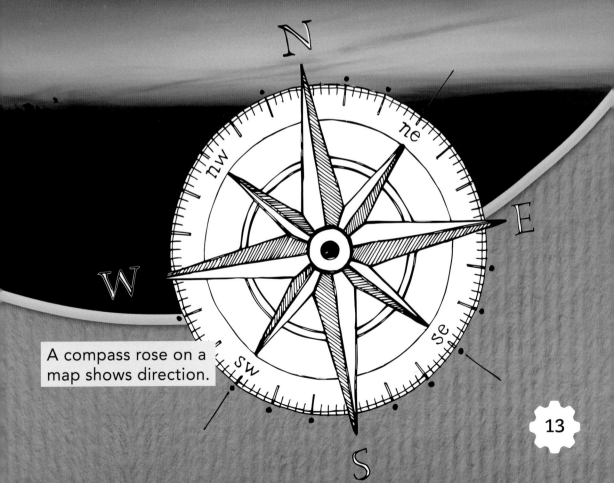

A compass rose on a map shows direction.

Slowly, maps have been filled in. But there are still unmapped parts of Earth. The biggest blank space is the ocean floor.

Scientists are trying to learn more about the ocean floor. They know it is there, but they do not know details. They are using **sound waves** to find those details. Ships send sound waves underwater. Scientists write how long it takes for the waves to echo, or bounce, back. That helps them know the shape of the ocean floor.

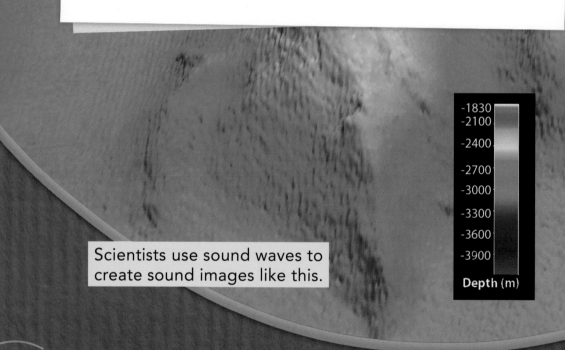

Scientists use sound waves to create sound images like this.

-1830
-2100
-2400
-2700
-3000
-3300
-3600
-3900

Depth (m)

How Sound Waves Map the Ocean Floor

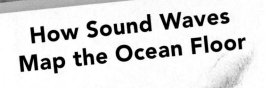

1 A ship sends sound waves.

5 Scientists record the echo time.

2 Sound waves travel down.

4 Sound waves travel back up to the ship.

3 Sound waves hit the ocean floor.

The View from Above

Most maps show a view from above. This is called a bird's-eye view. It seems as though people are seeing the land the way a bird would.

In the past, a bird's-eye view was hard to draw. There were no airplanes. People did not know what land looked like from above. Then, about two hundred years ago, people started buying cameras. They tied wires to them, and strapped the cameras to kites. They put cameras on balloons and birds too. People could use the wires to take pictures of the view from above.

U.S. Army members hold a kite with a camera attached in 1895.

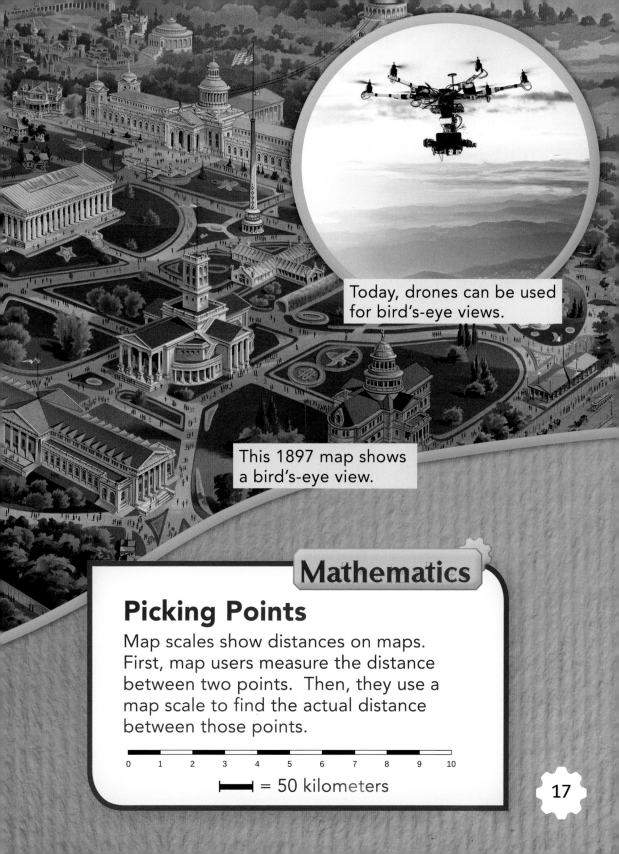

Today, drones can be used for bird's-eye views.

This 1897 map shows a bird's-eye view.

Picking Points

Map scales show distances on maps. First, map users measure the distance between two points. Then, they use a map scale to find the actual distance between those points.

```
0   1   2   3   4   5   6   7   8   9   10
```

⊢—⊣ = 50 kilometers

It used to be hard to take photos from the sky. But today, it is easy. In fact, photos are being taken from higher up than ever before. People who make maps can even use photos taken from space.

Astronauts who live and work in space take some of the photos. **Satellites** take some of them too. They all show what Earth looks like from far away.

This photo of the Strait of Gibraltar was taken from a satellite in space.

Astronaut Don Pettit uses his drill and camera to take photos.

Space Shots

Taking photos from space used to be a problem. They ended up blurry. One astronaut on the International Space Station (ISS) had an idea. He put a camera on a drill. The drill spun the camera the opposite way of the ISS. The spin kept the camera steady. It gave him clear photos.

The view from above has changed how maps are made. It is now easy to know the shape of a road or a river. And from space, people can see things that are hard to notice from the ground.

One example is in Africa. It is called the Eye of the **Sahara**. It is a huge circle made from rocks. The shape is too big to see from the ground. But high above Earth, the shape is **obvious**. Seeing the world from above makes maps more accurate.

Eye of the Sahara from the ground

Eye of the Sahara from space

Mobile Maps

Maps today are easy to use. Many people have smartphones. That means they always have a map in their hands. Maps today are very accurate too. Most are based off **GPS**. GPS is a tool that connects with phones. It uses satellites in space. GPS can show where a person is at all times.

A man in Thailand uses GPS on his smartphone.

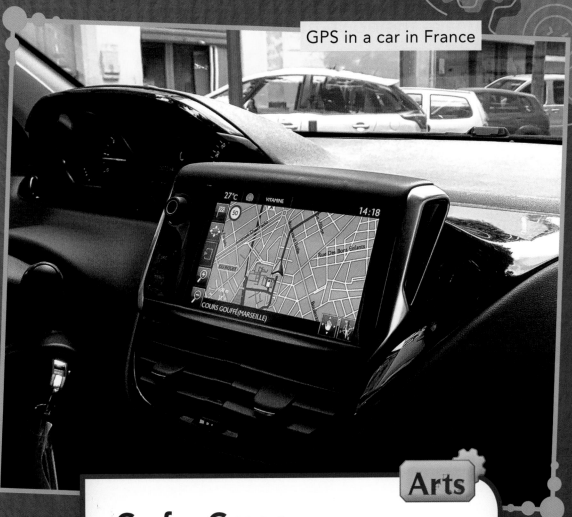

GPS in a car in France

Arts

Go for Green

Most GPS maps use colors to show **traffic** conditions. Green means traffic is normal. Yellow means it is moving more slowly than normal. Red (or black) means traffic is moving very slowly. These colors help people avoid heavy traffic.

23

Engineers are working on a new way to have cars make their own maps. Sensors on cars would scan roads and note all the rocks and bumps. These small details would be added to one huge map.

The map would not be for people to read. It would be a map made by cars, for cars. Cars that drive themselves would use it to give passengers a smoother ride.

A passenger sits in a car that drives itself.

This device makes a digital map of street and building details.

A self-driving car uses technology to drive safely.

Maps Matter

Maps really matter. Some people collect old maps. They spend a lot of money buying them. Other old maps are displayed in museums. These maps are works of art and science. They are important pieces of history, as well.

Today's maps are works of art and science too. They are not as expensive to buy. But they still help people find their way.

This image of Boston was taken from space in 2012.

This map of Boston was drawn around 1700.

This is a current map of Boston.

STEAM CHALLENGE

Define the Problem

A new student just joined your class. Your teacher has asked you to create a school map for the student.

Constraints: Your map must be drawn from a bird's-eye view. You must include color in your map.

Criteria: Your map must have a map legend, a compass rose, and drawings of important places at your school. It should be clear and easy to use.

Research and Brainstorm

How do maps help people get around? What will different colors mean on your map? What are the important places at your school? Where are they located?

Design and Build

Decide what you will include in your map legend. Then, sketch your school as though you were looking from above. Draw and color your map.

Test and Improve

Share your map with your friends. Ask them to find a place on your map. Did they find it easily? Is your map clear? How can you improve your map? Improve your map and present it again.

Reflect and Share

Could a new student read and understand your map? How can you make your map easier to follow?

Glossary

accurate—free from error or mistakes

compass—a tool with a magnetic needle that shows direction

explored—traveled to or studied

GPS—stands for Global Positioning System; a system that uses signals from space to tell a person where they are and to give directions

obvious—easy to notice or see

quadrant—a tool that is used to find how far north or south a person is

Sahara—a very large desert in Africa

satellites—machines sent into space to communicate with Earth

sound waves—vibrations that can be heard

traffic—refers to the amount of people or vehicles along a road or in a place